# THE

# KINGDOM'S

# TABLE

By

## APOSTLE ROBERT J. D. JENKINS

2 Tigers
LLC

*"Your words were found, and I did eat them;*
*and your word was unto me the joy and rejoicing of*
*my heart:*
*for I am called by thy name,*
*O LORD God of hosts."*

*Jeremiah 15:16 KJV*

# COPYRIGHT

Copyright ©2020 by Robert Jenkins

Printed in the United States of America

ISBN 978-1-945491-26-9

Published by 2 Tigers LLC


First Edition

# DEDICATION

This book is dedicated to Divine Insight Ministries and all of the precious people that listen and support the ministry daily.

To my wonderful wife, who is always by my side with a push and praise. Cassandra Jenkins, I'll love you always.

# TABLE OF CONTENTS

# INTRODUCTION

## How often do you eat?

This is a trick question. You may not know how often you eat until you know how you eat. You may disagree and say that we eat only by putting food in our mouths, but there are more ways to eat than by placing food in your mouth. You can eat with your eyes, with your ears, and with your mind. WOW! Now that makes the question more challenging. You would be surprised by all the things we consume through our eyes, ears, mouth, and mind. If you eat the right things, you will experience health. If you eat the wrong things, you will experience sickness.

## How much do you eat?

We eat all day and night in so many different ways, and we eat so many other things. We have become overweight because of junk food, and we still love it. We are fed by culture, television, cell phones, Facebook, media, church, jobs, family, life, and even dreams. We are addicted to eating, and many are sick because of it. Laziness and death are the results of consuming too much of the wrong foods. Adam and Eve committed the first sin by wrongful eating, and forbidden eating has not stopped since that day.

## Why is eating important?

If we do not eat, we will die. But what we eat and why we eat needs to be understood to make the right choices. Eating should replenish what was lost. What you eat should restore your body. We have a responsibility in hearing, seeing, speaking, and, most of all, thinking. How we eat also teaches us about our behaviors.

## How to Read This Book

*Thirty-one Plates* is a large Thanksgiving feast to feed your spirit and soul. Each plate is a different topic that will bless you. Please treat this book like a smorgasbord. Eat as much as you want until you are full of God's word. You may find yourself eating a little and then just sitting and allowing the Holy Spirit to minister to you. Eating the right foods brings you to the right place in your mind.

> *"Then Jesus said unto them,*
> *Verily, verily, I say unto you,*
> *except ye eat the flesh of the Son of man,*
> *and drink his blood, ye have no life in you."*
> *John 6:53 KJV*

I am only the server. God is the cook.

> *"Jesus answered them, '*
> *Truly, truly, I say to you, you are seeking me,*
> *not because you saw signs,*
> *but because you ate and were filled with the loaves.*
> *Do not work for the food that perishes,*
> *but for the food that endures to eternal life,*
> *which the Son of Man will give to you.*

*For on him God the Father has set his seal.'"*
*John 6:26-27 KJV*

Did you know that eating brings life?

> *"They that eat my flesh, and drink my blood,*
> *hath eternal life;*
> *and I will raise him up on the last day."*
> *John 6:54 KJV*

# CHAPTER 1: ROAST TURKEY

## Inside broken; outside rich.

We live in a world that is consumed with fashion and image. A person will walk in a room wearing thousands of dollars on his back at the expense of being broken, discouraged, and mad. We try so hard to keep up with the Joneses, who may be just as broken as we are, but hide it better. The things that we need the most-- like love, peace, character, and integrity--are not for sale. What matters in life must come from the inside. We have been wrongly trained to focus on the outside, and for that reason, we are made-up but not made over. There is nothing wrong with looking good and having nice things, but when our investment is a hiding place for insecurity and a poverty mindset, this becomes a big problem.

We invest in things that will spoil our souls and expire over time. We are afraid to look inward and see who we are and the potential we carry. This is a disease for which the world offers no cure, only more make-up. After years and years of this kind of living, a person will become frustrated. Such a person will begin searching for fulfillment, thinking that by obtaining more, life will become better. The "I need more" mindset will kill you, and feeling that you are never enough will cost you dearly!

Depending on external worth is the result of a slave consciousness. Thinking like a slave will rob us of our identity. A person who is secure in their identity doesn't need external things to feel valued. External worth teaches us to hide behind what others can see and what the world says has value. The real value comes from the inside place, which is the divine. The Bible talks about placing your desire in things above and not below (Colossians 3:2). We must, therefore, wake up to where real value and worth are and where they come from. Too many people are asleep, dreaming of the beautiful lie.

We need to ask ourselves some hard questions. Is this God's fault? What is life all about? Why is life about what we see on the outside? Genesis 1:26 says that we were created in the image and likeness of God. God is a Spirit, and Adam and Eve were created naked and not ashamed. As we acknowledge this reality, why then do we need so much on the outside instead of embracing our greatness on the inside? These questions are a threat to our ignorant, slave mindset and challenge our man-made happiness, but they are necessary. Can you hear the spirit of these questions? If not, you may be protecting the lie that you say you don't believe in. The truth does not need our protection. Truth from eternity can always handle a question from time.

God has already placed in us everything we need to help us live a healthy life. John 7:38 says, "Out of your belly shall flow rivers of living water." This flow is from within. Luke 17:21 says that the kingdom is from within. Kingdom thinking is the only right-thinking for a believer, and that thinking comes from within. You were created a king but born a slave. Therefore, you must be born again to receive the mind of a king, to eat like a king, and most of all, to think like a king. When we begin to see and know how rich we are from within, then our assurance of purpose will be revealed. Real value comes from both the invisible world and the invisible place.

When you value the external over the internal, you will become a slave to your possessions in order to keep them. But when you release greatness from within, then you become the possessor of everything you need. When you only value what is on the outside, you become just one of the crowd. Appreciating what is within makes you a leader of new pathways yet to be seen. When you get to this level of understanding, you will no longer need external validation. It is time to take your power back! What was given to you in the first place by God is worth so much more than what others say about you or what you wear!

# CHAPTER 2

## Practice. Preach. Power.

If you want your words to carry power, then you must practice what you preach. It's not always easy, but this is the truth. In my forty years of preaching, I could preach so well the very things that I did not practice, and the lack of power was evident in my own life.

The change came when I wanted to see this power and not just tell others about the power. I watched for years how the older saints in the church always had so much power in their words and their lives. What I found notable is that they didn't have to say much, but I could feel the presence of God when they testified. I have learned that the power behind words comes alive when we practice what we preach or when we only preach what we are practicing. If you are preaching something that you can't practice, your power is imprisoned by a lack of faith.

Sometimes we don't believe the words we say; instead, we believe the comments others have said about us, even when they are negative and untrue. Maybe the reason you can't practice what you preach is because of the word curses spoken over your life. Many times, word curses are activated by our personal beliefs. Sometimes what people are saying about you is what you already believe to be accurate, yet you get upset because you see that you cannot hide anymore.

We must discern the lies that are standing over us because of a lack of faith in what God has said about us. You can't change your preaching until you adjust your thinking. The ability to change the way you view things is how you have a more successful life. Thoughts are so important because they ultimately determine how your life will turn out. Praying and talking to others who can see you the way God views you will help you develop a habit of healthy thinking. We must discern how hidden values and intentions can control our behavior.

# CHAPTER 3

## Looking crazy while getting there

Sometimes following God by faith makes you look like a fool, but don't quit! When I was a little boy, I would walk to school with tears in my eyes, singing songs to the Lord that I made up. Everyone around me wondered what was wrong with me. However, I knew God's hands were on my life, even as a child. I was called to do His work, but my journey made me look crazy to the world. Just think about it, Jesus tells Peter to come and walk on the water, but as soon as Peter stepped off the boat, the wind became worse, and he began to sink. He looked like he made a mistake to everyone around him.

There are times when following God will create a crazy experience, but you know that it's God. Moses talked to a burning bush that wasn't being consumed. The Lord spoke to him through the bush. Now that's crazy! It's the crazy things that lead us to know God at a deeper level. The question to ponder here is: are you willing to trust God when things look crazy to the average eye? 1 Corinthians 1:27 says that God uses the foolish things to confound the wise.

Many times God will move outside of what we perceive as normal, but we must be convinced that what we saw and experienced is real. Never question a move of God because it is different from other people's experiences. Remember that it takes vision to pursue this crazy journey. Vision is about having eyes from heaven that bring things on earth to its rightful place.

Don't allow these so-called crazy experiences to rob you of great expectations. Let me encourage you by the word of God. Jeremiah 29:11 says, "For I know the plans I have for you, declares the Lord, plans for welfare and not for evil, to give you a future and a hope." And this is the truth even when it looks crazy.

Crazy experiences are training for the vision. Joseph had a dream that he was above his family but was shortly thereafter put into a pit. Sometimes to go high, we must first go low. To be great, we must first look crazy. Crazy training is really an invitation for God to prove to the world that He is behind you.

# CHAPTER 4

## Trapped in greatness

Can I be who I know I am, or am I trapped in greatness? That is a loaded question. Let's look at another question. Can I be who I am not? The answer is no, but often we try very hard to become that. The truth is not only who we are but also who we have become by not being who we were created to become. Now that's scary because I may love who I have become; however, I can't deny who *I am not* so that I can keep alive the person I've become. Most people never come to know *who they are* from God's viewpoint. Life and others can begin to shape you before the awareness of self is revealed and developed.

You may say, "Well, if I can become someone else, then I can be who I am not." No, that is not true. You can *do* who you are not, *but that's you doing and not you being.* Therefore, I say that you are trapped. You are trapped in two main places. Firstly, you are trapped in the false identity of who you are *and* are not. Secondly, you are trapped in doing *and* not being. Therefore, things have become hard. It takes so much work to fight the real you. Most of us go through life being told what to do but rarely who we are to be. And if you are trapped, then so is your greatness. If an apple seed is restricted because it's in a box, then the power to be a tree and its releasing of apples is also limited.

It's time for the leader in you to be revealed. The power that you need to be who you were called to be is in the choice to be exactly what God has declared. You can no longer do or be what people may want. Genesis 1:28 it says that God created us to have dominion and to be fruitful. This doesn't mean that we don't need coaching, but we must only receive from those God has placed in our lives to help us. All seeds have visions, and all visionaries need coaching. Coaching will help you become true to God's image and likeness. Take responsibility for your assignments and calling, and from now on, focus on who God says you are. Accept only the greatness that is in you.

# CHAPTER 5

## Laughing like a dummy

Sometimes when I am on Facebook, I see all of the foolery that we laugh at, but when something is significant, the post receives just a few likes. We are so damaged that we rather look at and share videos to make us laugh rather than to learn and grow. Don't get me wrong, there is nothing wrong with laughter, but let's not laugh at the expense of staying broken.

David did not take kindly to the laughter of Goliath. The laughter brought a disgrace to Israel. He said, "Who is this uncircumcised Philistine that he should defy the armies of the living God?" This same David would not give his brothers a chance to silence him. He asserted his right to speak his own opinion. Even though he was the youngest, he was not afraid of his older brothers! To make a difference, we must take a stand and be willing to face family and others who may be older but unwilling to fight. Later we will laugh at how they doubted the power of God in our lives to defeat the enemy. David said to Saul, "Let no one lose heart because of this Philistine; your servant will go and fight him." We need servants who will not only serve the king but are also willing to fight the enemy.

Let's look at some significant verses from 1 Samuel 17:32-37. In verse 31, Saul replied, "You are not able to go out against this Philistine and fight him; you are only a boy, and he has been a fighting man from his youth." Saul, an accomplished warrior himself, tried to give David a reality check, but David doesn't accept it. As David explained his confidence, notice that this isn't just bragging, but faith in God!

Many people will try to talk you out of your God-given assignment, but you must fight the things that you are equipped for by the Lord. David told Saul all that he encountered while protecting his father's sheep. David knew that he had been trained for this battle.

In verse 38, David said, "Your servant has killed both the lion and the bear; this uncircumcised Philistine will be like one of them because he has defied the armies of the living God. The LORD who delivered me from the paw of the lion and the paw of the bear will deliver me from the hand of this Philistine." Saul said to David, "Go, and the LORD be with you.'"

Consider David's experience. He had been a mere shepherd, but he had done mortal combat with both lions and bears. He was fearless! When his flock was attacked, he didn't take the easy way out. He chased after the predator, confronted it, killed it, and rescued the sheep from its jaws. Where are the David's in our day? Where are the fighters that are committed to the struggle? Where are the ones that will only laugh their way to victory, not finding humor in defeat? Laughter is not wrong, but make sure that you are not the joke. Sometimes we laugh because we have become hopeless. Who is laughing at your life? While you're busy laughing, what's going on behind the scenes?

# CHAPTER 6

## Laughter without tears

God has a way of making us laugh when people thought we would cry. The most remarkable experiences are those that have proven you are an overcomer. Remember when you felt that life was over, and then things got better? There were so many times that I was convinced that I could not make it. My pain was beyond repair, and then God used that very thing to make me stronger and wiser. He even gave me joy. These times changed my life and taught me that it is impossible to live healthy without having a renewed mind.

You will never have personal freedom and fulfillment without facing and transforming your fears into faith. These lessons will help you understand how to move with God's timing and not your own. One of the most powerful lessons that I had to learn was to accept what God has allowed and to know that His ways and timing are for my best interest. When you accept this truth, you can laugh without tears. You will have no regrets. The Glory of God can then be revealed in you.

Many people have experienced so much pain that they have given up on looking for a life with joy continually. Today it seems like all news is bad news. God has promised us victory, and He is willing to fight the battle for us. There is a story in the Bible that talks about a woman who was about 90 years old, and God opened her womb to conceive. She laughed because she thought that her time to conceive was over, but God had made a promise. Many of us are like that woman, but get ready to laugh because your promise is here!

# CHAPTER 7

## Prepared to carry the weight

You may not know it now, but you are being prepared to carry the weight for many people. Sometimes God chooses us to have strong shoulders. You have been made strong to help those that are weak. This is the reason you survived hard times so that you can help others through the same thing. Leadership is built by people who can handle adversity and then teach others how to do the same. When you can carry the weight of others, God will assign you to their troubles.

There will be many times that you will ask yourself how much should I get involved. Galatians 6:1 KJV says, "Brethren, if a man be overtaken in a fault, ye which are spiritual, restore such a one in the spirit of meekness; considering thyself, lest thou also be tempted." One of the strengths of being spiritual is that you can restore other people who are in need. This calling will bring you into a mature place. You will need to be mature enough to see where people are and help restore them in the spirit of meekness, knowing that you could be in this same place they are one day. Many people will need you to be there for them when things get rough and shaky, which is your calling and purpose.

Restoration is not about exposing sins or faults, but it's about knowing that wholeness is needed in the kingdom. We will not stand by and let people's lives be destroyed. You have been given a responsibility, so you cannot afford to become high-minded. God will call us to have the courage and stand up against the odds, especially when it's for someone else's benefit. Nothing's solely about us.

# CHAPTER 8

## Paying it forward

Life is about spreading the love of God to the world. When you come to understand that you only made it by the grace of God, your heart will go out to others that need to feel this love. This awareness will bring us into the understanding of God's unity. The grounds of God's unity are laid in the spiritual communion of each soul. The Bible talks about this in Ephesians 4:5-6 when it describes unity as "one Spirit," the "one Lord," and the "one God and Father of all." We are all family by the blood of Jesus Christ.

The central object of salvation, in a sense, is to reunite, to bring together again, to reconcile, and to restore the unity that God created before sin and the fall. Salvation not only restores men back to God but also men back to their brothers and sisters. You can't be a part of the body and not feel the pain of others and not be moved with compassion. Love becomes the burden giver and a healer at the same time. Whenever I help someone with a problem, this also becomes medicine for me. Just because we are free in God doesn't mean that the fight is over. We must join in on the war with others that may not be as wise or strong as we are.

The enemy is recruiting vessels from the house of God, and we can't just sit back and let this happen. If the love of God has not moved you to join in the struggle for others, then your love for God is being hindered by selfishness. Many people are on the journey of recovering from pain and suffering, which can be a lifetime voyage. Unity in Christ can bring us all to fullness. Pay it forward so that others can extend love to their circles.

# CHAPTER 9

## I was given to give

You are being shaped to be a blessing for someone else, so don't be selfish. I have learned to be thankful for my pain. I have come to understand the power behind the lessons that I learned. The hope that I received during and after the storm has become a potent medicine for others. This painful experience was nothing but an opportunity to help others come to a resolution. The worst pain and suffering is often invisible, and it will take the Holy Spirit and discernment to help you find where you need healing.

My most challenging life experiences ended up being a blessing to others. Now I know how to remain calm when "bad" things happen because I know they will work out for my good. Where you are as a person, spiritually and emotionally, is also where your ministry will be needed for those at that spiritually and emotionally are in that same place. This is the mindset that was given to me by the Lord from my pain to help others get through life.

Remember that the pain and suffering that you feel is only telling you how you thought and felt in the past. Your now self also knows the truth. The truth is that all things in life are gifts to us. These lessons polish us so we can shine like kings. It's a wonderful insight to learn that nothing happens to you, but all things can only happen through you. You are always complete, fulfilled, and whole. Any thoughts less than that are from the outside of the past or the future, and that's not where you live. You only live in the now.

Pain and suffering are illusions that seem real in their world. These illusions are using you to make them real because life is in you, and *without you*, pain and suffering will no longer be. This place is called heaven. Remove yourself from the world of pain and suffering and stay in heaven, which is now. Only then will you see complete love and freedom. There is only one place where you can be free, and that place is called love. God has given us the greatest gift: the love of the Father through His Son Jesus the Christ.

# CHAPTER 10

## Love will answer the call

Love will answer the call to truth, the truth which is Christ. Truth tells us that love is the only cure for all illusions, and only through illusion do we believe that there is a cause or a problem. Love is God's most significant investment. God's investment is to show oneness and never move you from the place of being. Nothing is added or subtracted from the place called love. This call is from the Spirit to show us how to smile even when we fall and to let not our hearts be troubled by the troubles we may have at the time. When it comes to God, nothing is ever lost.

It's funny how we say we trust God in all things and for all things. But when things don't go the way we think, we start living in the past of regrets or the future of hope. Pain has us always waiting for some great day. Well, the truth is, all we really have is right now. Wherever you are is where you need to be in order to complete your assignment at this time.

Decide to live in your "right now" moment, remembering that pain is only in your past, and hope is in your future. It is noteworthy to state here that freedom is in living; not complaining and wanting, and living is being free and happy right now. Life in God is about being free from all regrets. Say this with me, "no more regrets!" Now smile on purpose because of what you know to be true in your spirit. If the plan for my life is and will always be controlled by God even after my choices and God's plan will prevail, then why regret my choices when his will is perfect even in my imperfection. Love always answers the call to the whys in your life but for right now, thank God that you know that it is God's love and grace that are keeping you. God is trying to teach us how to have a breakthrough, not a breakdown.

The way you perceive a thing will determine a breakthrough or a breakdown. It is not what happens to you but how you see it and interpret it. When it rains, the farmer will rejoice, but the kids on the playground will be upset even though the rain was not at fault. So when it rains, learn to be content like the farmer. When it's sunny, enjoy the sunshine like the kids.

# CHAPTER 11

## Please touch me back

Being touched is one of the most important things in life, but it's also one of the most overlooked. There are also many ways to touch someone and to be touched. When a baby is born, it cries for the touch of its mother. Many people are lost because of the lack of being touched. We need to sound the alarm about the need to be touched and the need to touch back.

The emotional safety of the children is based upon how they are touched. These cries can't be ignored. Who and what touches our children shapes them. We live in a world that people no longer see the need to touch. This is an age of the cell phone, voicemails, and text messages, resulting in a great loss of personal and social connections. Without being touched, we lack intimacy with people and the ability to feel.

Many people keep this a secret, and this kind of secret will hurt you later. When you haven't been touched, it robs you of being able to touch others because you don't know what relating to people looks or feels like. Now this lack of touch causes you to live your life in fear. Your mind always tells you that you are in danger, and the very thing that you need, you now fear. This is also the reason many people settle for religion and not relationships because religion doesn't require a touch.

America needs healing by a touch. Our wounds as a nation are very deep. Until we as a people become healed of our spiritual and natural wounds, we will live in a world so close yet so far away.

Many of us have experienced some major things in our lives and need a touch from a pure place. Some of us have experienced mental, physical, sexual abuse, death of a child, or incurable disease, and from this experience, we never trust being touched from the right place. We need men and women of God to have wisdom in dealing with those who have been afflicted. How can the wounded become whole again? Many of us need healing in our minds because we blame God for allowing these things to happen to us. Others are like Cain, who would rather kill his brother than face his own anger. Many of us have cried out for help, but it seems as if no one is listening.

We have allowed race, color, religion, money, and many other things to separate us from real relationships. This separation has caused mental problems between us, resulting in us believing that there is no need to be touched. Subsequently, we have given up on touching one other in the name of protection.

Just like everyone else, the lack of being touched causes us to hold false ideas and thoughts. While some of them cause us very little trouble, others make us anxious, angry, guilty, depressed, sad and discouraged. The good news is we don't have to keep holding onto these false ideas and thoughts, which cause us to feel miserable and unhappy until we die. Did you know that most saints die unhappy and longing to be touched?

The first step in changing our unhealthy thoughts is for us to find them. That is not always as simple as we may think because many of them are held unconsciously. In other words, we are thinking these false ideas and thoughts automatically—that is, without realizing that we do so. Consequently, not only are we used to thinking this way, but this very thinking habit—like many of our other habits—is present in us without our knowing. We must begin to understand the need for a right touch and, like a baby, cry for it daily.

# CHAPTER 12

## Rejoicing from both sides

There is great joy in seeing people fly high when you know that they had to walk so low. Yes, someone supporting you in your victory is one thing, but for them to stay with you in your failures is another. It's so important to understand people on both sides. I can't really appreciate your fruit without knowing the story of your roots. People who are so full of hope may have started out with very little help.

There is someone who has been called to know and believe in you, someone who can appreciate the creative side of who you are. There is someone who can look behind the doors of pain and rejection and see the real you. There is someone who knows about the source of all your thoughts and will not say that you are crazy.

God will place people in your life that will never allow you to suffer in ignorance. They will remind you to ask

God for understanding and the purpose of your suffering. They will help you remember that suffering is the touchstone of spiritual progress. Never be blinded by the pain in suffering to the point that you miss the lessons and reasons for the suffering. Hope sees the real threats of absurdity, but it refuses to allow absurdity to have the final word about reality.

I had to learn that if my origin is insignificant, then my destiny and everything in between is also insignificant. I must see the purpose in all things and allow it to bring me to a healthy place regardless of the good or bad experiences that try to change me.

Each heart knows its own bitterness, and life will tell you that no one can have joy forever. Experience tells you that no one will ever completely understand you, and sometimes this seems true. You are so unique, and there are times when you may be hidden, but don't be shocked by this. Uncertainty about life is a normal thing but allows life to reveal all sides of your true self. Life's journey is purposed by God to help you come to know yourself.

Regardless of what life brings, remember that to move on and get up, you must look at things from all angles. A one-sided view of anything will kill you and will lie to you. In the Bible, Romans 8:28 says that all things work together for good to those that are called and love the Lord. These are keywords to apply to all situations, regardless of what they may be. Pain is a one-sided view, but so are joys, but pain and joy are called the journey of life. I encourage you to not live life from a one-sided view. Lessons come from all sides, and what you need to get to the next level is contained in both sides of life. We will gain authority and power from the lessons that we learn from both sides. You show me someone that is strong, and I will show you someone who has learned from all things. By faith, Moses stood in front of the red sea and believed God for a miracle. But this miracle was also while he was being chased by Pharaoh. Both sides of life will teach you how to stand over your red sea. Both sides of life teach you how to see the walls falling in your life. Both sides of life teach you what it means to be raised from the dead. It's by these lessons in life that I have learned to hear the voice of the Lord. Learning from all things helps you to be a better individual and to walk into your personal destiny.

# CHAPTER 13

## God's love never runs out

You may be tired, but you are not empty because God's love never runs out, and God lives in you. You have a well of love that is waiting for withdrawal by the people that have need of this love. Love is the strongest element in the world, and we are full of it. There are times in our lives that we would rather show hate than love. However, it is not your nature to hate, but to love. The foundation of salvation is love, and love is at its best when things are at their worst. Therefore, the Bible states that while we were yet a sinner, Christ died for the ungodly. We read in St. John 3:16 that God so loved the world that He gave His only begotten son. This is the greatest love story in the world, and it includes you and me. When the Bible says in Genesis 1:26 that we were created in the image and likeness of God, this means that we were created in love. We must not allow our weakness, emotion, and being offended to convince us that we are not loved or that we don't have any love to give.

God has a great deal of concern about loving him with all our heart, soul, and mind. And then he says to love our neighbor, as we love ourselves. When our passion is connected to the wrong things or persons, this becomes a misdirection to our purpose. When "love" is in rightly operation in us, it brings emotional safety to our loved ones. When love is not in place, then neither is healthy communication. You must understand that only by loving God can you detect your ego, and detecting your ego is a must to holy living and loving from the right place. It's the light of love that removes your ego.

Love seeks to find all darkness, covering, lying, reframing, defenses, abuse, excuse, blaming others, blaming society, blaming the environment, blaming childhood experiences, damning others, persecuting others, suppression, repression, whining, avoiding, and bringing them to the light. Love by design fills places that are empty and moves us to a still and quiet place in God.

Love flows, but wounds stop you from doing what is natural and easy. However, the strength of love will bring you to a healthy place and allow you to flow. Being wounded makes you question your place of purpose, but love reveals the why in your purpose.

It is so important to live a holy and sanctified life. Such a lifestyle will guide your heart to the things that truly matter. We were never designed to live on the sideline of our lives. There is a place in God where you live free from stress even when you are in stressful conditions. Stress is the heart killer, which hinders love from flowing correctly. All of these things hinder you from using the most powerful tool in the world called love.

My behavior reflects my mindset. It is because of Christ that I have a new mindset; not only about myself but also about others.

# CHAPTER 14

## Step and see

You will be amazed at what you can do once you start doing it. My mother told me that the only difference between one man to another is what he knows. If you learn what he knows, then you can do what he does. This has been with me for years, and I have taken this wisdom to the bank, but regardless of what you know, it will not get easier until you start.

Fear keeps us in bondage to ease things, and once we begin to see this, it becomes a funny flashback. There were so many things that I just thought were so hard, and once I learned it, I must laugh and say wow, it was this easy all the time.

Faith is another thing that we must look at to see and understand how we have made it across the distance to where we currently are. When I look back over my life and see how God allowed me to write many books, write songs, play drums, and the piano, and it was by having faith and believing in God. It's not just time to start doing but to start believing in your dreams. All dreams are done one step at a time. It takes courage and sometimes walking through your fears and then looking back and saying even you will not hold me down. We all must start somewhere, so why not start with what you love and have a passion for. Once you get started, things will begin to flow. The love that you have on the inside of you will guide you. You will look back and say, why did I take so long. There was a poem that I read that stated on the other side of fear is your blessing. Your blessing was waiting on you to get started.

*"The LORD had said to Abram, 'Leave your country, your people and your father's household and go to the land I will show you. I will make you into a great nation and I will bless you; I will make your name great, and you will be a blessing. I will bless those who bless you, and whoever curses you I will curse; and all peoples on earth will be blessed through you '(Genesis 12:1-3).*

Sometimes getting started is only hard because you refuse to leave and let go. Sometimes we are tied to the wrong people. Abraham was promised blessing, but he had to follow God and leave his family and his city. Where he was destined to go, his family could not get him there. This move required faith, and the hardest part about anything is walking where you have never been. The good part is that since you have never been there, you have nothing to lose, so start walking.

It's a very risky thing to leave behind everything that is familiar and go without knowing your destination. The concept of the family sometimes means everything to a person, but our destiny must be fulfilled as well. Another place where you must start is speaking up for your destiny and stop waiting on others to do what you can do for yourself. You must be prepared for the future and not let it pass you by. Time is always moving, but are you? You must start discovering your passion and reach deep down on the inside and bring forth all that you have been hiding and suppressing. This is the time that you step into your identity and show the world who you are and what God has destined for you.

# CHAPTER 15

## Looking through the eyes of love

When we look at people through the eyes of love, they will begin to change into better people in our eyes. Love will always bring truth to the picture and God's original intent for man. Love removes the baggage and allows you to see from a pure place. Love never just sees the dirt but the light from the diamond that is shining through. All mankind was created in the image and likeness of God, and God is love. Love's eyes are the only ones that can see the truth regardless of the behavior. This kind of love is what's needed in this world.

We all have been given the best gift in the world, and that is the gift to love. Most people put it down to pick up judgment and hate. Whenever love is not in place, people will be out of place. We must fight hard and long to keep love in its rightful place in our hearts. Love sees value in all things, and love is always in a sacrificial position. This is our God-given right to see all people through the eyes of love. When I look at the world and see its condition, I have concluded that the thing we most lack is the willingness to see and respond to all things from the eyes of love. Love must become like a vitamin that we take every day to have healthy eyesight and insight. We, as people, lack that great vitamin called love. How do we make judgments without love, because without love, judgment has already been made? Love is not for people only, but it's needed in everything that we do.

I am a musician, and I remember my brother telling me to never play music for money but always play out of my love. The greatest workers are those that love to do what they do. Love should be the motivator in all gifts and expressions. If you want to see your best, it will only be revealed by love being at the forefront. God is love, and when what you do is for and by God, then you will see God at his best. Love is the creator of all things, but love is the redeemer for all things. Love will raise that dead dream back to life again. Whenever you see things through the eyes of love, you see hope again, regardless of the failure or weakness.

Love will refuse to give up, regardless if it is people, dreams, marriages, and children. Therefore, the enemy doesn't want you to see anything through the eyes of love because it will put hope back in the game. Real hope is in Christ, and He wasn't defeated but defeated all odds. Love will reveal to you the strength that remains. In the book of Revelation, God tells The Church to return to its first love. We are not only to return to our first love but also to always keep that love first place. We were blind by the first fall, but by Christ, we can see again, and this came by His love for us while we were yet a sinner. God saw us through love even while we were in our sinful state. The Bible also says by loving-kindness have I pulled you in.

What love sees it also goes after? Love is an action word, and it can never just stand by without redeeming and revealing. People are waiting for us to see them for who they really are. We were born to love and to be loved. Love is a natural expression and a natural need. We all like being touched. The problem is that many things in life will hide or shape you into something else. But God has placed his love in the hearts of men that will always find you and help you to return to your true self. The struggle is not in seeing the value of people.

# CHAPTER 16

## Keep your doors open

Your house has become the hospital for many, so keep your doors open. God has trusted you to help people with their problems, and therefore you can't quit. If you shut your doors, many people may never trust God again. Sometimes we are the prayers and hope that people need to see. Therefore, you should be open to listening to people so that you can help them with their problems.

Many people will talk and come to you for help, so do not think that this is strange; it's just your calling. People feel comfortable around you, and they love to talk to you. There is something about your presence that causes them to just open up to you. My mother, before she passed on to Glory, had a difficult time sleeping at night. She used that problem as an opportunity to help so many people that would call her all through the night. We all need to see how our problems can become roads for others to travel to a better place.

My mother's doors were always open, and so many people are changed today because of her open heart to them. My mother was in pain all the time, but her pain made her accessible to others in pain too. You will be amazed at how God uses problems to lead to purpose. God may have chosen you to be his example of faith, hope, and love. You can't be selfish and abort your calling and assignment just because it becomes taxing at times. Your strengths will become leaning poles for others until healing takes place in their lives.

A friend of mine told me about a dream that he had concerning me. In the dream, my house was open to the world. People would come by, and the house was clean and prepared for guests. He said in the dream that there were empty baskets, and the host of the house would say to the guest it's ok to unload and talk because this house is for healing. This dream is not just my spiritual purpose, but you are as well; therefore, you are reading this book.

You will never meet anyone by accident, and every person you meet is for a reason, a season, or a lifetime. God is working on your attitude and awareness so that in these encounters, you can give them completely what is needed.

People are looking for a place to unload their frustration and leave you as a better and brighter person. People will need to trust you with their wounds and know that you have their best interests in mind. You were destined to show them the light and, at the same time, remove the darkness. Strangers will see you as their best friend. People will know that you are the one to take them to their next level in life. You were destined to be a people person and was given the love needed to function in it. Your time and money will be used in this ministry. You will always be thinking about others. God has given you more than enough of the things needed to help others that you don't even know; have yet to meet.

There is a burden that comes with this call, and many will not understand you. Many times, it will look like you are a fool and that you are easy to take advantage of, but that's all lies. You are not here just for you but called to help others. You may even struggle with this kind of love for others at first, but as time moves on, you will grow into it. It's crucial that you walk in this calling with confidence because it involves another wealth being. Being called may sometimes seem unfair to your wishes and dreams, but once you taste the joy of helping someone get out of a hole that it will all begin to make sense.

Thank you for joining in the struggle of others, and welcome to the life fight for others.

# CHAPTER 17

## I need your story

Wake up there is an emergency; people need your story. You have been through too much to keep it a secret. You can't be another person who adds to the graveyard. The graveyard is the place where dreams and ideas were never released. Too many people procrastinate and let time pass them by, and then it's too late.

Just like you are being blessed by my story, you will help people by sharing your story. I know that it will be painful, and therefore you must tell it so that others that may walk that road can have hope of how to escape.

Purpose is for problems, and your problems should wake up your purpose. Here are some examples. If you have a problem with bad teeth, then the purpose is the dentist. Let's look at another one. If you have a problem called chest pains, the purpose is the doctor. Wherever you see a problem, God has given a purpose and a person to solve that problem.

A lot of times, we become silent but sometimes help is not in just what you do but in what you say, write, paint, and many other things. The need for your purpose is in demand, but you may not know it until you reveal where you are and what you bring to the table. Every great person has a story, but everybody is not writing their story as they live. Why live the story and not share the story that you have lived? There are two many lessons in your story that the world needs to hear about.

Just imagine how hard it would be for Christians if there were no Bible. The Bible is full of stories of people's lives that reveal how to overcome and keep the faith. What's in your journey that would help people if they only knew the truth about your strengths and weaknesses encountered along the way? Not only is your story needed, but there is an urgency for this story. While you are procrastinating, people are dying. Don't you dare stay home or die with my medicine in your mouth! You must let the world know your suffering and your strengths. I am reading a book right now that is changing my life, and the person who wrote it is dead and gone, but because it was written, the medicine is still available.

Only you can write your story because only you can give us the truth from your perspective and your feelings. Your life has been touched by so many people, and you have touched so many people. Just as everyone has their own set of fingerprints, this is also true when it comes to the fingerprints on your soul. Your story will prepare us for the future and show us how to move forward from the past. Your story will be a coach for many and lead many to a better place. Your story will help people make better decisions by learning from their mistakes.

I know you may be afraid and don't know what to do but start by just confessing that your story is needed and will be released. How long will you act like you are barren when you know that you are pregnant with dreams, ideas, and purpose?

# CHAPTER 18

## Love is never out of a job

God's love is one of the most needed expressions in the world, but it is the most misunderstood expression of God. Love is a word that is used in all music styles. It is the strongest language in relationships, and everyone wants it and needs it. Love is always in somebody's life. When we come to understand the function of God's love, it will have you thinking that you are a fool. Love in nature is Sacrificial. Love is needed to wake people up to their own value. It says in 1 Corinthians 13 that love suffers long, and it endures all things. I always say that love will be overlooked and, most of the time, taken advantage of before it's appreciated. People fight against real love because it demands honesty and truth. Love is the real indicator, according to who you are in God.

Many times, we have been shaped by something or someone else, so when we meet love for the first time, it looks like an enemy. Love will fight you for the real you and not except the false you that is intriguing. The hardest thing to believe is that love doesn't have a selfish motive in loving you. It shows love because it is love. Love only gives you what it is. Love only does what it is, and that is LOVE. All your life, you must earn something to get something, so you struggle with believing that a gift is pure. It's hard when you have never had anyone to love you "just because" and you have never loved yourself "just because." This makes it hard for love to do its job, but it doesn't stop because this is what love is and what love does.

The lack of understanding of the function of love makes it hard because most of our experience of love is defined by what we do, not because of who we are. The main purpose of love is to reveal to us the value we carry. When this kind of love is introduced to us, we fight against it. When I look at the world, I see that in every place, love is needed at the forefront. Whenever there is a loss, a fall, a marriage, or even death, love is still needed in that area. I have come to see how blessed I am to carry such a powerful gift. There were many days that I hated having love for people that would or could not love me back. I didn't see how much I needed this type of love until I needed love that endured and suffered with me.

Then I saw the value of this kind of love while at the same time seeing the value of myself. I decided from that point on that I would accept my call from love to love, and I was prepared for the job. Love removes the blinders from your eyes. Love reveals grace and mercy freely. Love says no more barren womb; I will place what you need on the inside. Love refuses to allow living with a closed mind. When love is at work, your ear will open because the Bible says that faith comes by hearing, and faith works by love. Love also says No more closed eyes. This is when love reveals to you a spiritual vision and removes you from the superficial. Love will also allow you to speak from your heart and not just your head. I can hear love saying No more blood clot because it's my job to flow.

# CHAPTER 19

## When love refuses to leave.

One of the most astonishing revelations that I have received is the understanding of love. In first Corinthians 13, it talks about the commitment of love, which is beyond human reasoning. How do you come to understand something that endures all things? This kind of love is only understood when it is experienced. Learning about God's love was rewarding because God never changes; neither does his love. God is a covenant forming God, and his commitment is beyond our imagination. The reason love will never leave is because love knows and sees the value in a person. Love is determined to be revealed to you, and I want it to be known and seen in us. God's love will bring this value out regardless of the struggle.

Love is not like people who walk away when things get hard, but love will move closer. Love searches the heart of man, looking for its place of residence. God's love was designed to live in your heart, and when it is not there, you are living with a void. I am not saying that love will leave you, but I am saying that you may be stopping love from flowing. Regardless of the offense, love is saying, just let me help you and right there is that place. Love is not afraid to get its hands dirty. Love will work with you through all of your struggles and then work with you concerning others. Love sees all things as an opportunity to love. Love is faithful to the journey because it has vision and expectations.

There will be many times that you will have a shift in your feelings, but the truth about love will remain. Love is always on the inside, saying, "I am here, and I do have the answers, but you must allow me to flow." Just like the blood touches every area in the body, love must flow through all things. Love is designed to always bring you to a healthy place. Love is always communicating how important it is to be true to you and being in the right place and position. You have a very trusted friend, and his name is love. Without listening to love, you will never get to know the real you. Love is kind and is always honest. Love is your security system for the body. Nothing can protect you better than love. Our problem is not "love" but receiving and trusting "God's love" from the Holy

Spirit. In the Bible, it talks about how Jesus said to His disciples, that I now call you, friend. God is love, which means that love is our friend, and we must trust him.

# CHAPTER 20

## Touching God's way

Who knows better how to help someone than the person who created them? Sometimes leaders forget that before you joined their church or their ministry that you were already one of God's people. As much as you want to help someone, you don't know him or her as God does. The Bible says in Proverbs to train up a child in the way he should go, but you can't do the training until you know the way. You can't even help yourself without God's instruction. Life is about giving your will over to God, even when you have an assignment or a calling. This submission may seem unfair until you see the plans that God has for you, especially in the lives of others. It's easy to think that life is about you, but really, we are here to bless others.

When I look back over my life and see how many people I have touched just by being what God made me to be and no more, it is quite humbling. When we do things according to the will of the Lord, this will always be beneficial to others and you. Many times, you didn't even know that you were helping, and our biggest blessing is when we are not aware of it. The key is to keep saying yes to God and allow Him to use you. We were born to be vessels in the hand of the master. A vessel must be made clean and filled, but first you must be chosen. It's a blessing for God to choose you. When we really understand that God has chosen us to be used as a blessing for others, this brings a mindset of honor. You were chosen before the foundation of the world to be a blessing to others.

Therefore, he made you the way you are, and being true to you is a part of helping others. When we decide to be anything other than what God has designed for us, this hinders the path for others because until you become "you," there are things you just will not do. When we are not in our right position, the enemy takes advantage of this and hurts people while we are out of place. Just think about all the people that you were able to help and what would have happened to them if you were not in that place to make a difference.

Being true to you is so important when it comes to you being used as a vessel. The reason the cup is clean is so that whoever drinks from it will not be harmed. How can we help other people if we are not obedient to God? If the glass is in denial about being a glass, then the use of the glass is on hold until there is an awakening. When I am not in my right position with God, then I will also be in the wrong position with man. Jonah almost caused the whole ship to sink because he was in the wrong place, going to the wrong place. If many people can die by being in the wrong place, how many people will live because I am in the right place with God and man? One thing to remember is that when helping people, you are helping them become the way God designed them. Many times, people try to change you to fix their expectations, but this is not what we do. We help you to become the sons of God.

# CHAPTER 21

## Hope being lifted high

Life brings many struggles, and it takes courage and willpower to fight. The good news is that there is a victory if you don't quit. When you are going through, your mindset is to just get through it, but later, you come to understand how your life can help others. There is no greater story than the one that has helped others to cross over. People need to see others get up because we know about falls, but what about the strength to rise. It's time to tell people how you made it over and not hold back because many people may have to travel down that same road. Many times, because of the pain that life has caused us, we don't ever want anyone to experience what we have been through, but many will. You are not the only one that has been broken and left behind, but you are a survivor. Because of your testimony, they can have hope and a pathway out. People were depending on you to make it. There have been a lot of prayers with your name in them.

When I look back on my life and see how far I have come, I must tell the story. This is the reason I write so many books. I want people to know the pitfalls and the rises. When you read my story, you will be encouraged to fight on and never give up. My story gives hope to those that were raised in warfare by a single mother. I made it out of the ghetto, and against all the odds, I succeeded. I read a poem by Maya Angelo, and it said still I rise, against all the haters still I rise. Sometimes we are not aware of the people that are counting on us. When this day comes, they want to know how you do it. Are you ready to share? Are you prepared for the world to know your story? If not, then get ready because God did not allow you to overcome just for you to be alive. Many people have jumped off the bridge for the same things that you have been through and overcame. You must know how vital your purpose is to others. Also, the timing of your story can not be missed because too many lives are depending on it.

You are reading a book from a person who tried to take his life by taking pills. I also stood on a bridge preparing to jump, but now I am telling my story. You can never imagine how many people have been helped by my story and can also relate to my pain. Your pain is in the homes of many persons. When you begin to talk, it will be like you are reading their story which you are because your stories will be the same. Some people believe that no one can understand them but when you begin to speak, they will know that you do. Understanding their pain is the key to your story having a voice in their lives. The joy of knowing that your pain brings healing to so many is more rewarding and bigger than money. Your reward is to see another saved and restored because you shared your story.

# CHAPTER 22

## Sharing rather shopping

When you have been through the hard times like I have, it makes you take life very seriously. This produced in me a need to share the good news of Jesus the Christ with the world. I believe that time is too short to not share the love that He showed to us. Every day I carry a burden for the hurting, the lost, and the homeless. God has commissioned and anointed me to break yokes and raise the dead, heal the sick, and this assignment comes with a great price. There is nothing wrong with shopping and some pleasures, but when you have a burden, most of your time is spent thinking about or doing something to bring about a change.

When I watch the news and see all of the violence and innocent bloodshed daily, it stirs me even a greater way to do something. The cost of this assignment takes away a desire for a lot of pleasure and a lot of extras. I would rather use the blessing of the Lord on others than to live without the hurting being my concern. I am always giving and sharing so that others can experience life outside of debt and captivity. I read a book once that said that if there is anything in your house that you couldn't give away, then you didn't own it, but it owns you.

We live in a world that is so material-driven, and the weight of our appetite has been placed on the superficial. We are so image-conscious that the things that are important are lost. We ride past the homeless in our nice cars and believe that giving them some change is helping. It is not that nice driving cars and wearing nice clothes are bad, but when we receive our identity from things that we drive and wear, this is where the sin lies. We have lost our family to these things. Our children rather sit in the same room as us while everyone is on their divisional cell phone. Children are going to school with new and up to date phones, top of the line clothes while getting d's and f's.

The craving for these things has caused crime to go up and education to go down. Our children have a mindset to steal, lie, and do whatever to feed the craving of the materialism world. Where are the soldiers who are not caught up in "feed the world" addiction but are willing to sacrifice all to bring hope and freedom in all areas?

Our greatest problems are not pleasure and pain but the lack of truth, identity, purpose, and vision.

# CHAPTER 23

## Love have you seen it

Where is love? Where is God? These are the questions that are being asked from all walks of life. We have become a world that is driven by greed, lust, and control. When I look at sport arenas, the music industry, and The Church, I see where money is the driving force behind most of it. Many people talk about love and some of them are even searching for love but don't know how it looks. Love is something that all should have been born into but even that has changed. Many children were born into this world abandoned by their fathers and some were thrown away or freely given to the adoption centers by their mothers.

Love is a verb not a noun. In the Bible love is described in the form of charity because it's to be freely given. Most of the time we think that we are showing love but really we are making deals. One of the reasons God's love becomes challenging is because we only want to show this kind of love when we think it's desired. I remember when God was trying to teach me about his love. There were people that God was calling me to show his love, but I was looking for this same love in return. This became a problem for me because I felt like a fool to keep loving people who didn't choose to show me that same type of love. But God's love is not a deal or a tic for tac. God shows love because love is who he is, not just what he does. I must learn to love people based upon what God sees and not what I want from them. Love sees the value in people before they see it in themselves. Love always understands its assignment and is willing to go through whatever it takes to bring you to a healthy place. Again, the Bible says in 1 Corinthians 13 that love suffers all things and endureth all things and bears all things. There are so many people that need this kind of love, but are you willing to be this kind of vessel?

I talk a lot about love because it was my greatest cry but also my call from God to love. I went through life for many years, believing that I would never be loved for my worth. I also was willing to trade my act of love if you acted as if you loved me. I was ready to settle for the exchange, but love said you must love yourself and respect yourself. Love said I could love them if they never love me back. Can you stay complete in that, or do you need love on the outside to complete you? Love was teaching me about its function, and this was very hard for me to bear. I thought I needed someone else's love to be someone special or to have value in their eyes. When I learned that God is love, and I was made in his image and likeness, I stopped looking for love because, in Him, I am loved. The teachings from the Holy Spirit have helped me love people until they can love me back by knowing how rich they are in God's love.

# CHAPTER 24

## Solved problems must say thanks

There were many days in my life that I thought that no one needed me and that I was a person without purpose, but as I grew older, I found out that it was just the opposite. I had no idea the impact that I was making in the lives of others. The things that I was doing were small in my eyes, but to them, they were huge.

It may be years for someone to come back and say thanks but believe me, you are needed. When you do things out of the spirit of love, you don't do them with any expectations in mind. There are always outside voices trying to tear down the positive things that you do. If you listen to these voices, they will tell you that you are not needed because you can't see your strength, but it comes naturally sometimes, making these voices seem true. Most of us don't know our value unless we see where we are needed. Therefore, the little things seem to be overlooked. Many parents believe that their hard work was not appreciated. Sometimes it's not until later when their children are grown and have children of their own that they say "thanks mom" for being there for me.

If you are looking for people to openly thank you at once you may be disappointed. Don't allow this to define you as a loser or a nobody. Many great works go unnoticed until later in life. Sometimes you must be the hidden beam to a house, because you are the one that is holding it up and no one can see the hidden beams behind the wall. How many times have you heard people say this is a nice house, but they don't say tell the hammer I said thanks?

The key to life is to just stay true to your purpose and calling so that we can be fulfilled by your faithfulness to the cause. The Bible talks about a man by the name of Abraham who never staggered at the promises of God even though he never reaches them. Paul said that he fought a good fight and he ran the race and he finished his course. Abraham and Paul were true to their assignment, one reached it and the other didn't but they both were where God called them.

Waiting on people to see what you are doing will always place you into a personal delay. We must do all things for the audience of one and that one is God. When you do things out of the Spirit of love it also brings fulfillment.

# CHAPTER 25

## The secret must be told

The gold is in your mouth, so speak. Silence can be the foundation for wickedness. Many laws have been passed because the person who knew the truth didn't stand up. Many people have gotten away with rape, abuse, and many other things because you kept it a secret.

Your secrets are a threat to control and abuse. But what good is a threat if it doesn't show up? There are many ways to show up. They may be quiet while you are talking, but when you are done, you will receive a standing ovation. Remember that they are standing because you stood up. Not only is your story powerful, but it's also transforming. Many people are having private struggles, and they believe that there is no hope because you keep hope as a prisoner. You are not telling your story to hurt people but to free them from their own captivity. Your story is not just for your release but for those who committed the crime. There is freedom in knowing how you have recovered.

Many families have been ruined because of secrets. Many children would have a different way of viewing things if the truth about the family was revealed. God has given you the strength to handle the problem and to tell the truth.

My first book, *The Journey of False Perceptions* was full of secrets about me and many others. People would write to me and say that my book changed their life, but there were others who were upset about the family secrets being revealed. What people may not understand is that when you keep secrets, you also keep the ghost alive in you and others. Oftentimes secrets come with guilt and shame. These secrets can hinder you from moving ahead and committing to purpose and love because of the bondage that secrets keep you in. Whatever is kept in the dark is free to hide. The danger about secrets is that the roots that are growing but they are not seen. Many connections were not made even though the promises were given, but the secrets kept them apart. Therefore, when the Bible says that confession is good for the soul, this is a very true statement. Whatever you can't confess is also what you can't confront. Don't die with secrets that you could have been delivered from by the light of God, but chose to keep alive in the dark.

You don't owe anyone "the right" to keep you in bondage because of secrets that they know about you. I am not saying that all things need to be revealed to the world. I want you to consider what the secrets are doing to you while in the dark. The cost for the truth many times causes more pain than the believed lie. When it comes to secrets, do we say let the past stay in the past, or if we're honest can we admit that because of secrets, we are still living in the past? I advise you to never allow anything that was done to you or that you may have done to stop you from achieving what you can in life.

# CHAPTER 26

## From like to love

You never know the outcome of anything until it unfolds. People, friendship, and family are precious gifts. God knows how to bring you what you need to help you receive what you want. What may seem like an ordinary day may end up being the greatest connection in your life. The journey of life is fascinating and many times confusing but it does get better.

When I look back and see the people that I have come to love and how those relationships have grown, all I can say is wow! It's amazing how small things change into big things when you allow love to be the driver. Love always wakes you up to the greater and more. Liking can keep you stuck but not loving. The beauty of a journey is when you move from *I like* to *I love*. When you are in the like stage, surface things may have great weight, but when you are in the love stage, all things matter in its place. Love never allows your circumstances to have the last word. In the like stage, circumstances may change things, but in the love stage, circumstances reveal why love is there.

Don't give up before love happens. Always allow the journey to show you what was there; all you have to do is to just give it time. Like will bring us together, but love will keep us together. Like is what I want to live with, but love is what I can't live without. Like is what is formed the first time we meet, but love says I have always known you. Like can help my feelings, but love can break my heart. Love will bring you to a place of forgiveness and second chances. Like will help me to hear you, but love will allow me to know you.

There are many who I started out liking, but the more I got to know them, the more I loved them. I have a friend that says to know him is to love him. This same friend is afraid that when you first meet him, you will like him only because you don't know him. He says that the more people come to know him and see that he is always changing, then their thinking is that they don't like him anymore. My friend believes that most people may never come to know him and that his personality will run them away once they see just who he actually is. Sometimes we can't go from I like to I love because the transition needs too much work. Most of the time, we only like people that we agree with or those that agree with us.

Love is about purpose and understanding. Love says, let us not argue over which road if either road can get us to the same place. Love is committed even while hurting, but like will quit when pain shows up. There are some things that God has placed in your hands that you must go from liking them to loving them to see the best out of them.

# CHAPTER 27

## Pride the wrong investment

Pride will always protect the investment of what it claims to know, and your growth will always be stunted as a result. Pride is the number one thing that all people must work to eliminate.

Where there is pride, there is the devil's best work. God is the God of love, but pride is the thing that even God hates. Pride is an investor; you and I are the clients. If there is one thing that can cause a great fall; it's pride. Listening to pride will convince you to lie even to your best friend. Every fall has pride hiding its hand somewhere. Pride is also a traitor because it will push you out front but then leave you when you fall.

Pride is always after the first position in all things. It hates to be second, and it is never humble from a pure place. Pride will educate itself just to control everything. Even though it wants to be first, it doesn't want to seem prideful, and if it does, then it is because it has no respect for you at this level of being arrogant.

Pride is very disrespectful and laughs at serious matters because it's only concerned about itself. Pride is a bully, and it feeds on having all of the attention. We all must be aware of the spirit of pride. It has brought many great persons down. Lucifer was the worship leader in heaven, and pride got him kicked out. This prideful spirit is nothing to play with. Pride has no color nor race. It has convinced many people that it's the only way to be on top.

Television, media, and many other things have supported the spirit of pride. Many people think that without it, they can't be their best. I am not talking about pride in the positive way or the way of confidence. I am talking about pride that always believes that you are the best and will destroy you to prove it. I am talking about pride that is controlling. The Bible says that pride comes before fall. However, pride will make you think that others may fall by pride but not you. When you are falling, pride will give you a false sense of security and convince you that you have wings.

The same pride that took you over the cliff will make you feel so bad about the fall. Pride only stays around to get the glory and is never reasonable. Pride never takes responsibility for its choices when they have no glory in them. The voice of "pride" rarely speaks the truth because pride's voice only declares what it perceives as truth.

# CHAPTER 28

## When being right in showing love

We all have the right to love but should never love to be right at the expense of lying, cheating, and hating. It is better to understand than to be understood. The need to be right is also a position of pride because pride is selfish. It believes that love should only flow in one way, and that's to it.

When you struggle with identity being wrong attacks your character. It's not wrong to want to be right, but the need to be right needs to be examined. It's alright if you didn't get it right because now you have room to grow. However, what expense are you willing to incur in order to be right? Do you value being right more than being or showing love? Many parents can't show love because they must be right in their eyes at any expense. A person that must always be right most of the time will never say when they need help. Love will ask for help, but because the need to be right is coming from pride, it will keep your mouth closed.

How many great things have you walked away from because you needed to be right? It actually robbed you out of being loved? The best thing to be right in is love. Our desire should be to love right, stand right, give right, and pray right because the only right one is Jesus the Christ. The Bible says that there is no good thing in man and that our heart is wicked, so who can know it. It also says that there is a way that seems right to a man, but the end is destruction. Let God be true, and every man a liar. These scriptures should humble us and cause us to love right rather than always trying to be Mr. right in man's eyes.

The right and wrong discussion is a very old one and will always be at the forefront of discussion. The right to kill a baby, to carry a gun, to be gay, and the list goes on and on, but the correct question to ask is who God is. If God made the thing, then it is his right to set the rules. If God says it's wrong, then because he is the creator, then that makes his way the right way to live, think, and be.

The problem with America is that we don't use the same ruler in the same games. Slavery was never right in God's eyes, especially the way we did it. The way we think needs adjusting. We believe it is right to pay a person a billion of dollars to play sports but refuse to feed the homeless. We also believe that it is justifiable to kill a baby but not to fight dogs. Again, I say America has refused to repent because of its naive belief in it being right when it comes to the courses of action it takes.

# CHAPTER 29

## Repent

Every day I see where an act of my will could get in God's way. The trouble that we are in as a country is due to getting in God's way. However, this type of thinking has caused me to repent many times. It's a great and divine thing to have free-will, but I must not allow it to keep me in bondage. Remember that doing things your way will always bring you into bondage. If my will is not in line with God's, then I will be a stumbling block to me and others.

It took me a long time to know that I was not even suitable for me. When you are young, you think you know about life and what's best, but the truth is that you are immature and living in the dark. When you take things into your own hands, it says that we have more confidence in our way of doing things than we have in God's plan. We get in the way because we think we know what's right when often we don't. Just because God called you doesn't mean that you don't have confused days.

The question that I need to ask is this: what did you do when you were confused that was not in the will of the Lord? One of the hardest things for leaders to admit is that sometimes we don't know, and sometimes our help is a hindrance. Life is a journey, and we are all learning as we go. The power of choice is a good thing but sometimes a bad thing too.

When we start to think that we know better than God, then a big fall is waiting to happen. God has a perfect plan for imperfect people, but sometimes our gift makes us feel like we have it all together. Be very careful that the crowd doesn't take you out of the will of God. Doing things God's way is just using wisdom. God is the maker of all things and the creator of all people. Who knows better than God? This takes a while to understand because, from a human perspective, we think we know what's best or that we can make it work. It is important to note here that nothing works well outside of its design.

The true purpose of our will is to line up with God's will because he designed us to function a certain way. When Adam sinned in the garden, he not only became lost to God but also to himself. The mindset of Christ is the only way back to knowing God's will and plan for our lives. The difference between help and hindrance is understanding the goal and the vision of a thing. The plan that God has for us is beyond what we could ever imagine. Doing things God's way allows the world to see divinity on earth. This is man's original purpose. You want to be your best, but without reading your divine instruction, you will always function in dysfunction.

# CHAPTER 30

## Rare moments at anytime

God wants to use us in rare moments, but we must yield when these moments call. God wants us to be aware of them when they come and not run from these miraculous moments. We must be ready and never judge these moments the wrong way. God sometimes works in strange ways, so our hearts must be in line with the Holy Spirit. Turning the water to wine is a perfect example of this. When the men said to Mary, Jesus' mother, that there is no wine, her reply was, do whatever he says. There is an obedience that is needed to be an instrument in these rare moments.

You have been in training for these moments, and you know it. Therefore, stay motivated by your faith and not be hindered by your fears. Life wants you to think that you're alone in what you're facing. You may be hearing and seeing things that are far beyond your understanding, but that doesn't mean that you are off. The fear of the unknown is what prevents us from walking by faith into the known that was once unknown. If we're living for God, he is present no matter what is going on in our lives. God is the creator, and he is always creating in you, and I. God created everything by the spoken word, which means that when he is speaking, he is creating, and God is always speaking. The Holy Spirit is gentile, so we must be sensitive to the touch of the Spirit.

When doing kingdom work, we can't afford to be fearful. We must ask God to give us a broad vision concerning his purpose in the kingdom. Accepting God's assignment will always make a peaceful warrior out of you. Many people miss the perfect timing to see a miracle because it looks like a regular day. Jesus was a master of making everyday moments rare moments for the kingdom. Jacob went to sleep on a rock but later realized that he had entered a divine place. Moses thought he had just picked up a stick along his way on the ground and later found out that this stick was the rod to lead God's people. Paul had what we called a road of Damascus experience, and this experience changed his life forever. There were women who went to a well to get water but saw a man sitting at the well who was Jesus. All of these examples started out as normal days until they were made aware of the divine and rare moments. The people in the Bible are no different than you and me. There are many God moments that we will be awakened to.

# CHAPTER 31

## Don't waste a God opportunity

When people need you in their time of trouble, take it as an opportunity for God to show his love through you. It takes a sharp eye to recognize a God moment. God is trusting you to see him in all things and then present him to those who don't. All of God's moments are wrapped up in love. Love is never blind to any moment.

When you are looking through the eyes of God, you will see him. We must learn how to step into such moments ready and able to help as God reveals. God wants to use his love through you to demonstrate a miracle. We must trust God enough to act in these times of need.

We are given authority and dominion on earth to help people experience freedom in Christ Jesus. By faith, you will stand over the red sea in your brother's life. By faith, you will see his walls falling. By faith, the Lazarus in your life will rise from the dead. By faith, you hear the voice of the Lord says, keep loving and loving and loving. By faith, our personal destiny stays. By faith, we DECLARE AND ACT on the word regardless of the person's condition.

Let's imagine the joy of the Lord when he sees what we are willing to do what we can for our brothers and sisters in the Lord. That moment when we are eager to be like young David in the Bible, killing the Philistine giant and removing the disgrace from our brother's mind. This is the attitude that we take when it comes to our brothers. We are willing to say who is this uncircumcised Philistine that he should defy the armies of the living God? The word will get around that there are people who aren't afraid of Goliath. We have been called to fight alongside our brothers and sisters.

There will be a time when your phone will ring and on the other end will be a person very upset and very confused. It is your passion for people and training from the Holy Spirit that will cause you to bring them to a better place. Your anointing will break the curse and the yoke in their lives. You will not be upset because they interrupt your day, but for you, it was an honor to be called. There is no greater joy than to love and care for people.

God has taught you his purpose and plan for your life, and it's a great joy to serve. The greatest positions are son ship and servanthood.

This book was designed to feed you in your spirit and mind. Please allow the Holy Spirit to take this food and not only fill you up but also cause you to be pregnant. Come and sit down with others so that you can begin to pass around the plate of wisdom and knowledge gleaned from this book.

# ABOUT THE AUTHOR

Apostle Robert Jenkins lives with his wife, Cassandra, in New Orleans, Louisiana. They are the founders of Divine Insight Ministries, and Apostle is one of the trustees of the ministry called In My Father's House.

Divine Insight Ministries is a multicultural, Bible-based, spirit-filled ministry that engages in reaching the hearts of mankind, by first introducing their hearts to God.

Apostle Robert Jenkins has many years of Bible training and has traveled throughout various parts of the world during his 38 years of preaching. He has a revolutionary ministry gift and is known for revelatory preaching. He continues to share a God-inspired word, which is in high demand by both clergy and laity alike.

The command by God on Apostle Jenkins' life is the awakening of oneself to the truth. His endeavor for God's people is that:

- Purpose is revealed.
- Passions are renewed.
- Principles are restored.

"I believe that the key to every believer is knowing that the truth comes from within. God bless,"

*Apostle Robert J. D. Jenkins*

**Please leave a review on the website you purchased this book from – thanks so much!**

Connect with Apostle Jenkins and Divine Insight Ministries on social media.

Facebook

@DivineInsightMinistries

@Robert Jenkins

Instagram: @DivineInsightMinistries

www.ingramcontent.com/pod-product-compliance
Lightning Source LLC
Chambersburg PA
CBHW072022060426
42449CB00034B/1750